Free Indeed

by

J.A.Williams

AuthorHouse™
1663 Liberty Drive, Suite 200
Bloomington, IN 47403
www.authorhouse.com
Phone: 1-800-839-8640

This book is a work of non-fiction. Unless otherwise noted, the author and the publisher make no explicit guarantees as to the accuracy of the information contained in this book and in some cases, names of people and places have been altered to protect their privacy.

First published by AuthorHouse 7/28/2008

ISBN: 978-1-4343-9390-6 (sc)

Printed in the United States of America
Bloomington, Indiana

This book is printed on acid-free paper.

Acknowledgements

First and foremost I want to bring glory for my life to Jesus Christ, the one who has truly set me free from a life of sure endless misery. Second, (and she is second to none), my wife Candy who is the most up-front and honest person I have ever met. She is the definition of "virtuous". My mom, who is Mother Hubbard in her own right. She stands as the matriarch over the family, (you're beautiful inside and out, needless to say). My siblings, they are irreplacable, (what you see is what you get). The " old man", (you have more people looking up to you than you might think). Sher, (I hope there are semi trucks in heaven, you'll need one for all the jewels you're going to have). My Pastor on Sunday, and Wednesday and my Pastors on Monday. You shepherds are imparting more than you'll ever know. The Hill-Brayton-Leiter-Kimble Connection, what a back-up family you guys truly have been.

Introduction

I have written this book simply because the Lord has led me to write this book. I don't know all of the details as to who is meant to read it, but God does. It is an easy read (for those who don't like to read, or can't read well). It is basically a small read about my life to christians, and non-christians. It will also be a great read for those who suffer from any hinderance, or disability. God has a purpose and plan for every man, woman,and child. I hope this book encourages you to seek out God, and His blessings will seek after you......Matt. 6:33- But seek ye first the kingdom of God, and His righteousness and all these things shall be added unto you......

Chapter One~
Life as I knew it........

Childhood, everyone remembers their childhood, I do anyways. I can't say my childhood was horrible as some were, but it could've been better. I remember the little things about my childhood. Such as my older sister (yes, my sister), being a brut. She was rough, rugged, and always ready. Ready for whatever. This was my stepsister I am speaking of, we had a pretty big family growing up. Six kids in all, the Partridge Family in size, but definitely not in loving kindness towards each other. My family was mix-matched, like a lot of families in America today. My mom had myself and an older sister from her first marriage. She met a man who had a boy and a girl from his previous marriage. In 1977 they were married, and there were four of us children. The same year they had a boy, my little brother Billy, who today would remind one of Larry the Cable Guy. In 1982, they had a girl, so there were six of us, 3 boys, three girls.

Life was normal to me growing up, it had its moments, but alcoholism in the home didn't help matters. You don't always feel the effects of alcohol until years later. It did affect me, and I lived to tell about it. My step-dad was a tyrant, he didn't like many people and many people didn't like him. He didn't care that they didn't like him, he was his own person. My mom saw something in him, and we never figured out what it was. He was abusive (more so verbally) and we never figured out what the attraction was. He was a hard man to like, and he made it obvious he didn't like me when I was a kid, he just didn't show any love at all toward anybody. For whatever reason, he had a cold heart, toward lots of people. I did have some good times with my dad though. I recall a big fishing pond we had on our property, and the whole family enjoyed the pond, and all the critters we had around the farm. We were from the backwoods truly, and I believe we all would have chosen to stay there, now knowing what the outside world can do to people, especially young people. The Amish have the right idea, they farm their lands, live off of it and mind their own business rarely see them caught up in any mischief, rarely.

I don't blame to much of my past on anybody, because as I got older I accepted the decisions I made. Living in North Carolina as a young child was a good thing. Up until the age of 12 my family lived in North Carolina, literally in the country, no harm there, not then anyways. At the age of twelve my parents decided to move to Florida, Panama City to be exact. Boy, was I getting ready to grow up fast. The city was an awful place for someone like me, I was looking for attention, And I started finding it, in all the wrong arenas.

By the time we had moved to Florida, my older brother was already out of the home. He was basically sent to live with his real mom, because he was getting into trouble in the home, stealing, lying, just being a delinquent. I have only seen him one time in the past 20 years.

My older sister, the brut, moved away after graduating high school, she was military bound,we thought. She ended up moving to California, and met a man that had other things in mind for her. Like, for instance, just being his wife and nothing else. She has told us thru the years that he was abusive and used drugs and alcohol. That was in 1986, just about the time I was beginning to learn about this world we live in.

Florida was a good place for senior citizens to retire, yes. But it was no place for a young man like myself, one who had the sense for being curious, and I became curious.

I was in the seventh grade when I first started using drugs. Just about anything I learned was available and I quickly met people who were willing to give it to you, sell it to you, trade it to you, you name it. It was available. I gradually snowballed into petty thieving, some more serious than the other, still thieving nonetheless. My parents were getting baffled by my mischievousness, they simply didn't know what to do with me. My mother worked more hours than the average mom, and I didn't see her much growing up. She was a retail manager for many years, and it required her Presence at work. My dad (step-dad) worked as well all of my childhood, but for many years he consumed a lot of it, drinking. I gathered, looking back that my mom worked hard to try and get ahead, it never really worked as I was growing up. We didn't have a lot of extra money. We didn't go hungry, but we didn't have any extra.

As my junior high school days carried on I was skipping school, hanging out with the wrong crowds, just not having much care in the world for anyone, or myself. I was just existing, with no concern with what I was doing to myself or others as I went along. Something was wrong with me, I was doing things with no thought of what I was doing, I didn't have any understanding of what I was doing or the repercussion of my actions. Today, counselors like to label it as bi-polar or adhd, or whatever. And truthfully speaking I had some of those characteristics or thoughts. I just didn't know what to do about them, and back then neither did my mother. She tried to find some help for me, but everything cost money, big money, so I went without because we didn't have big money. In other words I was a product of society and society was raising me the same way it is raising kids today, like heathens. I even told my parents if they spanked me I would turn them in, in so many words. That is wrong with kids today, the parent doesn't have control, and the ones who do don't know how to parent, that's society. I had a behavioral problem definitely, and more, I learned as the years went by.

I was running away from home just to do it, I was looking for something, I just didn't know what I was looking for. As I have talked to people over the years, I have pinpointed what that something was. It seems everyone is trying to find their way. That's what I was doing. SO, I ran away from home, searching. What ended up happening is I found the law. The laws of the land that is, and I learned how to break them. I began by stealing and selling drugs, small amounts in the beginning , a users quantity I call it. As everyone else, I started with marijuana, slowly graduating to the elicit drugs. Not really having a care in the world I would lie about it every time my parents confronted me, but it was obvious at times. Like an addict, when I didn't have it, I was ornery. I wasn't exactly a full blown addict, but I was a user and abuser. I finally was sent to live with my maternal grandparents back in North Carolina. My folks thought I could get more positive attention from my grandparents, plus financially they could provide a better environment for me. I soon realized that my grandparents were spoiling me and I liked it. I always had pocket money to buy my marijuana and pills with. After a few months there in school I started getting into trouble as well. Just lying about stuff, staying out drinking and skipping school. I was up to no good basically. I didn't really have any concern for even myself, I had no clue what I was doing to myself. But, my grandparents were good to me.

At the end of my ninth grade year I was sent back to my parents in Florida, my grandparents couldn't exactly deal with me. I started my tenth grade year for a month or so then I told my mom I was dropping out of school and moving to South Dakota. I will always remember the day that I told me mom I was leaving home. She was hanging up clothes on the clothesline outside and she told me at that very moment that I would either end up dead or in prison. What in the world is in South Dakota you ask? Well, I had me a little ole job training dogs and I was ready for life on my own. So, I left.

The job was great, I was a greyhound dog trainer. I literally made over 500 a week, that was good money for a 16 year old. Wow, I was on top of it. I found out who all the drug dealers were, and the state of Iowa was just a few miles away. Back then, the state of Iowa was the methamphetamine capital of the world. I always needed meth to keep me awake because I worked long hours. Hey, like everyone else I had a reason to use drugs, right. SO, I used and abused for the whole summer of 1990. I was with my crowd of choice, all the losers. I fit right in. I remember one spell where I stayed awake for over a week and a half, on drugs. I was on a downward spiral. Finally, after a couple months of that, I was becoming irresponsible and my employers knew it. They fired me, and I was now homeless. Being homeless brings out the character in one, or should I say, builds character in one. I was stealing every meal I ate from the grocery stores. I would just walk in and steal some beanie weanies, or a pack of bologna. I even walked into a shoe store one time, tried on a pair of hiking boots and kept them on, not paying for them. I ran out of the store and never got caught, I was desperate. I eventually met a guy my age at the local homeless shelter in Sioux City, Iowa. We partnered up and started breaking into places at night. I became a part of a burglary ring, there were five of us involved. I didn't know any other life, really, but to survive at this point. Something was wrong with me. But what.

Chapter Two~
Twas the night before Christmas

I stayed around Sioux City for a while, I didn't have any other place to go, I was truly homeless. I was committing burglaries at an alarming rate, to this day not knowing how many I was a part of. On Christmas Eve Night, 1990 my buddies and I decided to try and break in to a car lot, the building itself. So, on Christmas night, we did just that, we broke in to the car lot. I guess, from what my court documents told me back then, we stole 7 or 8 cars that night. I ended up getting arrested, laying in the bushes, in an ally, beside a Catholic High School. I tell you these things because, the details, because I would end up reaping what I sowed. I learned that my group and I also broke into the Catholic School as well. I was found passed out in some bushes, on Christmas night, and it was one of the coldest nights on the books. I was fortunate to be found, or I probably wouldn't have lived through the night. I was actually thankful to be put in jail, shortly thereafter, juvenile detention, because I was under age. This beat the homeless shelter I was in and out of, no one was laying around drunk or trying to panhandle off of me.

It was great, to some point. I was glad just to have three hots and a cot, compared to being homeless. I got close to the other residents (inmates) there, and I learned in my first three days there that I was facing 85 years in prison, and the prosecutors were going to try me as an adult. I was bewildered, not knowing what to think exactly. I just didn't know what to think, I just went with the flow.

The prosecutors offered me a 25 year sentence in exchange for my cooperation. Not to snitch on anyone, just to cooperate and tell them of all the burglaries I had committed, just to help them solve some of them. I didn't agree. A 25 year sentence for someone like me was just way too much to handle. A 25 year sentence for a non-violent crime was too much.

In a couple of months the prosecutor offered me a 20 year sentence. I felt that was too much as well. I hung around the juvenile hall for a few more months, finally offered a 15 year sentence. My public defender told me this would be my best bet, to accept it, and he told me I would be released from prison in about 18 months. I thought, compared to some of the other cases I had seen, that wasn't too bad of a deal. Of course, who was I, I didn't know any thing about the law anyways.

On September 7, 1991 I was transferred from the Juvenile Detention Center to the Iowa Classification Center in Iowa City, Iowa. I was with the big dogs now. That was my eighteenth birthday present, going to the joint. I was housed there for three months before being transferred to the Iowa Mens Reformatory, the big house, for real. It was quite the experience my first few days, it was like being in a movie or something. I was not a happy camper, this place was a haven for filth and utter disgust. It was like a little city inside of a city, behind 40 foot limestone walls, a cage. It looked like a castle from medieval times really, and it felt like one, almost haunted. I took it all in, I fit right in with the other thieves and clientele. Lots of young men my age, just wandering around playing cards, hustling each other, and living the best way they knew how. I took to the gambling scene very well, it was my lifeline. After all, I was living against all odds anyways.

I was growing up in prison, many do these days. Lots of young people end up in prison and it doesn't seem to be a big deal to many. But, it is a very serious problem to some, some Americans make attempts to reach " in " to the prison population. I pray this book reaches in.

Chapter 3~
Denim Jeans and Pull~on shoes

The attire in the pen was a joke in itself. Everyone wore state issued blue jeans and pull on sandals. It made you feel like a loaf, a bum really. Some inmates had personal clothes if they could afford it, I wasn't one of those. I had to hustle literally everything I owned, by gambling, playing cards, I gambled on everything, including the weather. I would wager some high stakes at times, just hoping I didn't lose. At times I lost big, but winning more so, just fortunate. I fell right in to what society had sent me away to fall into. I was even dibbling and dabbling in the drug scene in the joint. People don't believe it, but yes there are drugs in most penitentiaries, really. I was fascinated with the amount of money people would pay to get their hands on the stuff, anything, pills, pot, anything. But, I tell you, this place was the devils playground. You know all the stories, some stories of prison are true. In my case, this prison was borderline compared to some other pens. There were fights, rapes, riots, attempted escapes, the norm for modern day. I just did my time for the first two years, minding my own business, hoping to get released when the parole board reviewed my case.

I finally came up for review in 1993, and no one was on my side. The parole board (and my caseworker) told me at that time that I needed to do more time. That was all they said, to do more time. Funny isn't it? My attorney told me that I would be released in 18 months. Well, that didn't happen. As you know, he was a court appointed attorney. I was jailing at this point, just jailing.

In 1995 I was up for another review, and the parole board granted me a transfer . A transfer to a medium security prison, to undergo drug treatment. Drug treatment; for what? I had been locked up for four years, and they wanted to send me through drug treatment before I was released.. They were accustomed to doing that to everyone, for some reason. Its funny how my parents couldn't find me any help prior to all of this happening, but it's in place for you once you get there.

I wasn't there long, I was doing drugs while in drug treatment, marijuana mainly. I was selling it for the most part, and gambling. I was sent back to the reformatory to serve out some disciplinary time, lock down in other words. I was in my cell, for 24 hours a day, only to get out for a shower every other day, for six months. That built some character in me, I was really learning by now. I didn't care too much for that type of stuff. Bad enough being locked up in prison, but prison inside of prison was even worse. I was beginning to get some understanding about life, some wisdom.

In the winter of 1997 something was wrong with me. I basically started having some delusional thoughts, weird thoughts. I don't recall all of the events, all I know is I ended up in the psychiatric hospital inside the prison. Now this place was not the place a person wanted to be, there were some strange folk on the mental ward. Really strange. I was seen by a doctor, interrogated basically, and at the time I was diagnosed as a paranoid schizophrenic. Yes, that would explain some of my earlier behavior, I was weird. I lived in the ward for about a month and was released back to general population.

Upon returning to general population, I was beginning to get back into some sort of contact with my family, my parents etc. By mail, by phone. I hadn't spoke to any of my family for 6 years at the time, I didn't know if they were dead or alive. My mom and I really smoothed over some of our differences, and let by-gones be by-gones. SO, in 1997, the summer of, my parents drove from Michigan to visit me in prison. This was the first time I had seen them in over seven years.

I explained to them my diagnoses and we settled on the thought that this could have been part of the reason I had made some of the bad decisions I had made in life. Behavioral problems could've stemmed from the illness. Who knows. All I knew was I was thinking abnormally at that time, and I did notice it. The parole board didn't do anything, they assumed that the medication that the prison psychiatrist had me on was all the treatment I needed. I never really felt comfortable with either the psychiatrists there or the medications. I was still "weird" no matter what they did with or for me. They would tell me what my problems were just be looking at me, not actually evaluating me.

On the psych ward I met some really interesting, and bizarre people. One man I remember as if it were yesterday, I'll call him Joe. This man was dying, physically. He had a disease like that of muscular dystrophy, but it attacked the nerves, he was literally bed ridden. I remember him for a couple of reasons. One, he used to give me his bowl of cereal every morning at breakfast time. I enjoyed the abundance of having two bowls of cereal. Also, he told me some things I had never heard before. One day we were sitting around the ward talking, just he and I . He asked me, " Do you know Jesus". I said, " No". I had heard of him. He said, " All of these problems you have, Jesus can solve". I was telling myself, "Pal, you don't even know the extent of my problems". He said, "Are you saved". I said, " Saved ? What does that mean?". He said, " If you want to get to know Jesus, just bow your head and say this little prayer with me". Basically the prayer was asking God for forgiveness of all the sins I had committed in my life, and I asked God to make himself known to me. That was it. He ended by saying, " You'll be saved". I said, "Saved from what?" He said, " You'll know when the time comes". I had no clue what he was talking about.

The characters I met on the psych ward were of different walks of life. Many to me seemed to be the type of people that no one really cared about at all, I talked with a lot of them. There were people in there with some major mental issues, and it was the most uncomfortable place I had ever been in my whole life. One inmate on the ward was pacing around the ping pong table shooting at whatever people he was imaginatively seeing. This was a place like no other. I had to get my senses collected so I could get out of there. The prisons psychiatrist told me if I beat him in a game of chess he would let me out of the psych ward. Was he out of his mind or what? To tell a man who was on heavy psychiatric medications if he beat you in a game of chess you would let him out of the psych ward. I remember it clearly.

Chapter 4~
That little lady........

As I said earlier, I didn't have any family coming to visit me. For that matter, I didn't have any contact with any of them. I did have one visitor on my visiting list while I was in prison. The lady I am speaking of was actually a youth leader at a local church back in Sioux City, and she used to come teach bible lessons to the offenders in the juvenile hall I was in. This same lady kept in touch with me through the years, coming to visit, writing me letters. Coincidentally enough, when I was transferred from juvenile hall to prison (on the other side of the state) her and her family moved within 20 miles of the reformatory I was in. She used to come sit with me for an hour or so, and tell me she was praying for me, and so on. I didn't quite get the gist of what she was praying about, or to whom.

I did know this, every thing happens for a reason. I now know that this lady was in my life for a reason. Today, I know all the reasons why she was in my life, it is all clear now. I still to this day am in frequent contact with this lady and I have told her that everyone I am ministering to today is accredited to her. She literally prayed my salvation (my walk with the Lord) into existence. She tells her church often of my week to week process, even 17 years after the fact. She says many of her church members still remember when my life was broken into pieces. I have told my friend that when she gets to heaven, there will be jewels in her crown for the ministry she has done in my life. And as I state here in this book, if anyone tries to force the "Living for God" on you, they are out of line. I say that simply because Jesus didn't do any of that, and neither did this lady. I would chat with her in the prison's visiting room, or by phone or letter. She would reply, quietly saying, " I'll be praying for you."

If there is someone in your life even remotely close in character to this lady, seek out their wisdom and yield to what they have to say. You won't be disappointed in the end. And you will remember that person forever............ She is still ministering to young people this day.

Chapter 5~
You live and learn............

I was released from prison in February of 1998, to a work release center. I had to go through the rigmarole of basically more incarceration. The center was a place where us "residents", (they didn't call us inmates there, we were residents), had to find a job and work our way back into society. I guess I of all people was grateful, I didn't want to be homeless like before. So, I took advantage of the situation and found a decent job. I was also doing lots of community service, voluntarily. Coincidentally enough, one of the places the director of the center asked me to speak at was a Catholic high school. I was seeing some interesting things unfold in my life, I tell you. After a seven year stretch in prison, I was ready to be totally free. You value freedom more than anything once you lose it, and I wasn't planning to lose it again. The thing I took to heart most, and the thing that made me want to change is this: I was jailed for too long, and I missed my freedom. I wasn't rehabilitated, I was jailed. That's sad to say, but it was true. I served literally seven years for a non-violent crime. A lot of people over the years have told me that serving that much time is absurd. I kind of thought the same thing.

I was seventeen years old at the time, and I was the youngest of all of the people involved in my crimes, so I feel the same way. But as I said earlier, everything happens for a reason, everything. Even the unexplainable.

While I was in the center I made contact with an old girlfriend of mine who happened to be living back in Florida where we had dated when I was in the eighth and ninth grade. I thought to myself that this must be destiny because we were sweethearts back then, surely we can pick up the pieces as adults and make a good relationship out of all of this. We stayed in contact during my entire stay at the work release center there in Iowa. She even flew up from Florida to visit me as soon as I was released. You know how it goes, I thought she was a "catch" and I fell head over heals. I found out shortly thereafter that this was one of the biggest mistakes I had yet to make.

I eventually ended up transferring my parole to Florida to be with her. We got married right after

Christmas, in January of 1999. We were living our lives as " good people". Not necessarily Christian people,but on the outside we were good people. She even held her employment at a local church there in Panama City. SO, people thought we were Christian people. She was in fact a closet alcoholic, and I was soon to discover that.

We lived together for about two months and it just didn't work out, I couldn't figure out why exactly. It was always a constant arguing arena, she was very contentious, loved to argue. Here I was just trying to live a little and enjoy the basics of life, freedom mainly.

I recall coming home from work early one evening, and she was sipping on some wine. I stood outside the back door and called her on my cell phone, and looked through the backdoor window as she sat there drinking. I called her on the home phone and told her I was on my way home. She hurried up and started shuffling around to hide the glass she was enjoying a drink from. I waited outside for a few minutes. I went to the street and got into my truck and pulled around to the front of our place. I acted as if I didn't have a clue what was going on.

During that time as well I would find bottles, beer bottles, wine bottles, full, half full, in the linen closet and other places. She was basically a closet alcoholic, and very contentious. We had our disputes, she didn't understand that she was a drunk, and I didn't try to explain. (I am not sharing this to defame anyone, I must say.) We split up for a week and I moved to Michigan where my entire immediately family was now living. My parents took me in, and they were glad to see that I was staying out of trouble. This was the beginning of my walk with the Lord Himself.......

Chapter 6~
Whom the Son Sets Free............

Michigan is a cold place. But, if you get in with the right people it can be quite quaint to live here. My parents had become church going people, I was unsure what I was. Upon arriving at my parents home, my mother asked me a question that really stirred me up. She said, " Are you saved.?" I said, " Saved?' I asked myself where I had heard that before. She asked me was I okay with going to church with them. I said sure, why not, my wife and I went to church occasionally. However, I was about to encounter God in a way I had never experienced before.

Since my release from prison I had stopped taking all of my medications. I felt that I could cope without medicine. After all, I felt that the psychiatrists in prison weren't qualified to give me a proper diagnoses and I would just live with my problem. Everything was normal, until I was at my parents for a few weeks.

I was depressed, not just psychiatrically speaking, but physically. Something came on me like nothing ever has. I know that my separation from my wife was a big factor, but there was more to this. This was spiritual, and dark.

My dad told me one evening before he and my mother turned in for the evening to get down and pray about my wife, give it to God. He said be sure to ask forgiveness of your sins, then ask the Lord to intervene in your situation.

I had said a prayer a few years earlier, but I didn't have a clue what it meant. I did however need God, something higher than myself to intervene. So, I got down beside the couch and I prayed, simply, but desperately. I said, God, if you are real, then show yourself to me, in my life. I felt a presence behind me that was very authorative, very authorative. For the first time in my life, I felt like my life was in someone else' hand. And it was. As I stayed there, knelt down praying, I was reminded of all the situations I had gotten myself into over the years, narrowly escaping. I remembered experiences inside and outside of prison. This person behind me was Jesus, the one I have heard people talk about. Without saying a word, he told me that He had already been in my life. I was seeing it all right before my very eyes, in visions, being repeated, of events in my life. As I said, this was a spiritual battle. One minute I was so depressed I couldn't even concentrate, the next I was in the presence of God himself.

After a week or so, my mother noticed I was getting really weird. I can't remember a whole lot of the weird episodes I was having, its unexplainable. I do recall my mother asking me one day if I needed to see a counselor. I agreed, and she took me to a local psychiatrist in a nearby town.

I sit in the doctors office for awhile answering his questions, unsure what to say or how to explain the thoughts I was having. I just don't remember all of the conversation, not any of it, to be honest. I do remember him dismissing my parents and I and giving us a prescription for me to begin.

I went ahead of my folks and I made my way toward the parking lot to get in the car. Rather than get in the car I just kept walking, and walking, and walking. I didn't know exactly where I was. I didn't even know I was missing from anywhere. I was just walking, along the Lake Michigan shoreline, and the boat docks that are there in South Haven.

My mother could probably write this chapter because her and my family remember more of it than I do. She tells me that I walked out of the doctors office and vanished. She says her and my dad didn't know what to do, so they rode around town looking for me. I didn't know I was lost, so I wasn't looking for anyone, I was just walking. After a few hours my parents went home, called the police, reported me missing,and called some of the members of their church. The church they called was a church they used to attend in the middle part of the state of Michigan.. She says people just started praying for me, that I would be found, and be found safely. She says after she spoke with a certain elder of the church, she felt relieved. She said the elder asked the Lord to send forth ministering angels to keep me safe, and she said she suddenly felt at peace. This is another act of God, and how He works. Through all of those years God was working in my parents lives, and mine as well, and here we were years later seeking Him together. My parents were exactly where God wanted them to be during these times, there for me. Truthfully, this was one of the most critical times of my life.

Eight or nine hours later, I remember walking past a fire station, and a cemetery. Something about the cemetery drew me towards it. I remember clearly at this time, seeing literal beings around me. And I could hear them, fluttering, wings fluttering. They were digital in nature, not fully in the physical realm, and they were ascending and descending. At that time I heard someone call my name, I looked behind me and it was two police officers, outside of their squad cars approaching me. I didn't understand what they were doing looking for me, but I complied to all of their requests, and they took me to the station.

While I was there they explained to me why I was there. They sent me to a local hospital for evaluation, and I was admitted for psychiatric help. I never did tell anyone about the angels that I knew I was in the presence of. They would add that to my list of problems, they simply wouldn't have understood. And some reading this book won't relate to it either, but some will.

I remained in that hospital for about two weeks, a lot of it I don't remember . I just know I was finding myself separating grandiose thoughts from actual spiritual happenings. My first night there I recall getting beside my bed to pray before I turned in for the night. I was on my knees facing the door entrance that led into my room; I could see the hallway and the lights therein. I seen, what was nothing to be described but angelic. I seen a character, in a illuminating robe, with a sword planted in the floor in front of him. This being was so tall that his head wouldn't fit into the hallway. In other words, it was as if his head went into the ceiling, because he was so tall. I have never had an occurrence like this, not even close. I knew at that time that this was Michael an angel, spoken highly of in the bible. I knew what it was and I wasn't nervous. It was as if he were sent to monitor me, wouldn't surprise me, knowing what I know now.

After those couple of weeks I was released on medication, and I was rediagnosed as being manic depressant. They have a name for everything. Basically I was suffering from depression, due mainly to my separation from my ex-wife. So, I was released back to my parents house.

A week after being out of the hospital my wife sent me divorce papers, with no explanation. She just wasn't willing to get any counseling for us, or anything of that nature. So, I took it to the Lord. Lord, I am on the verge of getting divorced, I will sign these papers. Lord, I pray my next wife is the opposite of the one I am getting ready to divorce.

One month later the divorce was final, and I was a divorced Christian man. Some think this is out of line, to be divorced. I do too, but it happened. I stayed single for two years, just enjoying freedom from prison, freedom from any major responsibilities, and life was good. I was free from prison, free from relational bondage, and free from the psych ward. God was showing Himself to me, taking away some things, and adding some things. My mother has to relive my child hood as an infant, she literally had to babysit me back to health. She had to see to everything I did until I was back in touch with reality. She had to cook my meals, give me my medicine, the whole nine yards. I stayed with my parents for a few months and moved a few miles away from them. I worked a maintenance job for a local apartment complex, stayed to myself and kept attending church. Still searching.......

Chapter 7~
Free Indeed

As I said I was enjoying my freedom, and enjoying spending time looking for God everywhere I went. I had a desire to discover what God had in store for me, now that I was getting to know Him personally. I found a relationship that was very pleasant . I had met a lady at the church I was attending with my parents. It truly started out as just a friendship. We were both Sunday school teachers, and we would enjoy one anothers' company away from church. She had an interest in cooking, and I had an interest in eating. So, we hit it off pretty good. Lots of people frowned on our relationship when it started taking a turn for more seriousness. Mainly because she is several years older than I am. We didn't ask for any ones opinion, except for the Lords. We recognized at the time that the Lord does have a sense of humor. This lady was a correctional officer in the state prison system in Indiana prior to us meeting. Yes, a sergeant, and a counselor . And here I was finding myself interested in her, really interested.

We dated for over a year before we pursued marriage. We were married in October of 2001, and God has been good to us. Life has had its challenges, but we managed.

I was still dealing with this illness though. I had a hard time focusing on anything I began, even employment. The slightest change in my work environment would rattle my cage. I had held a number of jobs, none really drawing my attention. I had something inside of me that needed to be fulfilled and my wife and I were determined to find out what it was. I had a lot of faith in God, but I wanted to know what He had planned for me. But yet, I was still dealing with this illness. After just three months of marriage I had lost my job I had when we first got married, getting laid off, the company went out of business. I was struggling with my parents separation, and a few other family issues in our life. The depression was still there, and it wanted to overtake my entire life. I had no clue what it would attempt to do, or that it was " ruling " over me. My wife did notice that I was acting peculiar, not really knowing what to do or think. What ended up happening was that my mother and my older sister drove across state to come stay with us for a week, to make an attempt to get me level-headed again. The three of them made every attempt to get me professional help, to no avail. They took me to a psychiatrist appointment to have me hospitalized and they tell me today that I " snowballed " the psychiatrist. This particular doctor didn't see any need in hospitalizing me. After a week of getting nowhere my mom and sister returned home. My wife says she was in absolute shambles, not knowing what to do. My mother told my wife that if I " took off" that she would have to call the police. Sure enough. I had told my wife one day I was going to go outside and walk around the yard. I ended up going for another one of my "walks" alright. My wife later told me and my family that she looked outside and I was long gone. She called the police and reported me basically missing. She informed them that I had been having some struggles and was being treated for depression. I myself didn't even know I was missing, I wasn't even functioning in reality, I was having what doctors called an "episode". There is a name for everything these days. Way back when people used to call in the priests when a person was having difficulties, not a psychiatrist. So, I was walking around the countryside along country roads and the only thing I really remember is a police officer pulling alongside of me. He asked me who I was, I told him. He said, "

Your wife is at home worried about you, and she wants me to check on you. Apparently I told the officer that I didn't have a wife, I told him that she was my girlfriend. I don't know why I told him this, I just did. He left me there where I was at walking down some country road. It happened to be the coldest day on record for that time of year, it was far below freezing. I ended up walking back home and climbing into my truck, my wife was out and about with my Pastor looking for me. Plus, they had went to the local mental health clinic and filled out paper work to have me found, and committed to a hospital. My wife says this was the hardest thing she had ever done in her life, having me committed. After hours of walking around the countryside, I was back at home sitting in my truck waiting for my wife to come back home. My pastor, his wife and my wife pulled into the driveway. They called the police again from there and told them I was back home. The police came to my house and picked me up, and took me to the hospital. I was completely oblivious to what was going on. I just wasn't living in reality. I had stayed in the hospital for a few weeks, and eventually came back to reality, not really remembering much about any of those events.

We kind of got a little off track for a few years, just "attending" church. Not really seeking God for what He wanted out of me. In 2004 we moved from the Lake

Michigan side of Michigan to mid- Michigan. To be closer to family, and to attend the little church that was praying me out of situations I've mentioned herein.

I had always told my wife that I knew God had a plan for me, a mighty plan, a specific plan. I just had to seek Him and find out what it was. One evening while having a talk with my wife,(we were asking the Lord to give us some guidance), He really spoke to us. I walked in the house from the back porch, and opened up a Christian magazine we subscribe to. It opened to the very last page. Interesting enough, there was an ad there, right in front of me, saying " Do you want to write a book, do you want to get credentialed?". This is my book, and I am presently in my second year of ministry school, aiming to be a licensed minister. I have been a youth leader at our church for about 3 years, and I love it. It is my heart, (it is also God's heart), to counsel and teach youth in a way to show them that I understand where they are at in life. It is also my primary responsibility to lead them down the road opposite of the one I took. But, I knew there was more. I just kept my day to day routines the same, being sure to visit with the Lord in prayer and devotions daily. I applied to a ministry school in Lansing, about 20 miles from my house.

As I said earlier, the Lord does have a sense of humor. I spoke to the pastoral Dean of the school, he invited me up to see the school and meet his wife. When I pulled into the parking lot, I could not believe my eyes. The building was made of a limestone type of stucco, much like the reformatory I was housed at for seven years. I just chuckled, what a transition my life had taken. All glory to God. I don't like looking back, and God isn't one to bring up your past or throw it in your face, but I am well aware of where He has brought me from......

I was anxious to begin school, real anxious. I am not 100 % sure where the Lord is leading my wife and I. But, I know this, we'll follow Him.

On December 10 th, 2006, I was at what I thought seemed to be a normal Wednesday night church service. We worshiped to a few songs, and the Pastor gave an altar call, allowing people to come to the front of the sanctuary to be prayed for . I went up front that evening, not out of the norm for me. I was standing there praying just seeking God about a few matters and a couple behind me started praying on me, I could feel there hands on my back. After only a few seconds I was overwhelmingly overtaking by the power of the Holy Spirit, I was laying on the floor . I laid there for what seemed like twenty minutes, and I could feel the presence of God just all over me. The man and woman told me that they knew something was wrong, but didn't know what so they just started praying. I told them at that time that I had been dealing with psychological depression for several years. After that night I haven't been on the drug Lithium, a medication I had been on up until that evening for seven years. Something was removed from me that night, and I have never been the same. That night I was once again set free......

Chapter 8~
Miracles never cease

My wife and I had experienced many miracles, living for the Lord was becoming a pleasant lifestyle. I was to begin ministry school in January 2007, the past few years were wasted in my eyes, I had some catching up to do. I want a career, and the Lord has one for me. Don't get into school and then want a career, you'll have one once you finish school. I have found myself trying to jump into some jobs that " seem " to be interesting, only to find out that isn't Gods plan for me at this moment. I do odd jobs, and a lot of volunteering while going through school. I want to share something that totally stood out to me. In October of 2006, prior to the Lord leading me to go to school and writing this book, I had attended a church service at a church here in town other than my own. I was basically just visiting. Well, while there the pastor of the church called me forward and started speaking some things into my life. The Christian folk like to call it " propheising". He told me, and I remember clearly. " I see you around a lot of black people". I said, " Okay." What does that mean, I asked myself. He then said he seen the word, "world changer". He asked me did those words mean anything to me. I couldn't think of any thing lining up with that. Well, I ended up contacting the school and they had sent me some information by mail. I opened up the envelope and a brochure was inside. On the back of the brochure it read, " Do you want to be a world changer". Interesting, but not a coincidence. I pulled into the parking lot of the school, as I said, and I was beside myself about the structure of the building. I went inside and met the pastor and some of the instructors, the majority of them were black. I have been blessed by being a part of this school, God knows it. I was once again in awe about the prophecy that God had spoken into my life. It had come to pass, and quickly.

Some people don't see a miracle for what it is. Miracles happen constantly. You are a miracle.

I have seen some miracles, healings, and wonders,. I have seen some things that have had me in a total awe state of mind. Only God can perform the unbelievable. The reason I have entered into a deep relationship with the Lord these last few years is because He can do things no one else can do, the unbelievable. That isn't the only reason, but its nice to know that the God I serve can do more than just be called a God. He is real, I tell you He is real. It is Gods desire that all men come to get to know Him, all men.

Other miracles have taking place, just little stuff that people take for granted. I'll illustrate a couple of things quickly here. So, here I was on my way to beginning ministry school. I was lying in bed with my wife one night, and I made a request of the Lord. We were really pushing it in our finances, we didn't have much money to run on that week. I said, " Lord, I need a book bag, for my books". I needed one, really, to go through school with, just a small request. I went to work two days later at a local pregnancy center where I volunteered . I was sorting through some clothes and a bag caught my eye hanging on the wall. It was different than the other bags it was hanging with, it was a bookbag. I picked it up, it was perfect for what I needed. I said, thank you Jesus. Then I looked at the label, it read " One Step Ahead". See, God is so faithful, so faithful.

I can go on and on about little details, daily blessings that God bestows upon my wife and I. We have seen God do whatever He wants to do. The biggest thing to me is that God knows that people like surprises, He is always giving me little surprises. He knows what we like and don't like, He is personal, if one lets Him be.

Around that same time, my wife and I called our pastor over to our apartment. We were stretching our money as far as it would stretch one week, and we had a decision to make. We had our tithe to pay and we had our car insurance that was due that same week. We said, " Pastor, we always tithe, but we've never been in this kind of predicament, what should we do". He said he had walked down this road before and he learned that God is faithful, but we ultimately have to make our own decision, to tithe or make our car insurance payment. We tithed, and let our car sit. One day before our car insurance actually ran out, we received enough money in the mail to make that car insurance payment, from out of nowhere. You tell me....

God is a provider, the Bible says clearly that the birds of the air don't worry about what they eat, and the Lord provides for them, so why should his own people really worry about their circumstances. I tell you this day, God has a plan for your life, no matter where you are at in life, He has a plan. And rest assured, it isn't a bad thing. Lots of people seem to see God as a disciplinarian. He is, but he isn't one to bring pain and suffering upon His people just to do it. He is a deliverer, a healer, a provider, first and foremost. Get an understanding right now that

God wants to be in your life, one has to let Him in. Yes, there are some things we all have to change in our lives to honor the Lord as we begin to walk with Him. But, He takes us just as we are.

Many other miracles, and unexplained occurrences have happened in our life as we have walked with the Lord. I am giving the reader the opportunity to decipher these things for themselves.

Another miracle that was nonetheless a miracle was this. The youth group I am involved with has seen many miracles, lots of them, as has our whole church. But, this was cool in my eyes. We

were fund-raising, as a youth group to go to a concert type of event as a youth group. It is a pretty big shindig, many have heard of it, its called Acquire the Fire. Well, us leaders have been trying to encourage our youth to get sponsors, each kid needing a minimum of $ 220 to be able to attend

this event. One of our fund-raisers was a Valentines Banquet, put on by the youth themselves, for adults. It is a nice dinner, where the youth sell tickets to couples, to assist them in going to this big event. We have really been encouraging the kids to step out on faith and believe God to bring in the money they needed to go to this event. At the banquet, where the youth served the adults their dinners, a man at the event asked one of the girls in the youth group, " How much more money do you need to meet your goal of $220 for this upcoming event . She said, " Oh, about $170. Right before the gentleman left for the evening after the banquet he handed the young lady a check for $170. This is simply God, doing what He loves to do, bless His people. This young lady was asking God for herself, and God opened a door for her, He responded to her by blessing her via this man that attended that evening. Miracles are what God does, that's just it. One should not think that the miracles I mention are all about money, I have some other ones I am going to share here.

One, there is a couple in my church who have struggled for years financially. Really struggled, the man of the house was laid off from one of the best jobs he ever had, and things were just not looking good for this family. They have two children, both who still live at home, the oldest of the two, a boy, is living with autism. My wife and I lived a few houses down the street from them for awhile and we used to go over to their house and fellowship. They had been stuck in a apartment, a ran down apartment for 13 years, never really being able to afford to move, anywhere other than there, just because. The wife had been really wanting to find them a house that they could afford to buy, not knowing if they could get financed or what. I, along with my wife and several other friends had told this lady to step up her faith, and start seeking God. After all, only God can make the impossible possible. She had a mutual friend of ours run their credit and see if they could get financed for a home. They did, they got approved for a loan. The loan however was only for about $ 60,000, and you just aren't going to find much of a house for 60,000 around where we live. A fixer-upper maybe, but that's about it. She began looking into foreclosure homes, which just anyone can't buy unless you're at the right place at the right time. The wife found one, for 47,000, and they moved forward to use the loan to purchase it. While the family was waiting for the loan and paperwork to go through, their only vehicle broke down. It really broke down, practically irreparable. Their paperwork went through and they ended up getting the home, several of us guys from the church moved them into their new home. Not even a week from the time they moved in did the same man that got them the financing, bought them a van. He said he felt led of the Lord to buy them that van. Isn't that something? God is real, very real. The bible says clearly that God will openly reward those who diligently seek Him, that's what it says. And that's what He does.

This past summer my wife and I had really put a lot of our finances towards helping her daughter (from a previous marriage) get settled in from moving here to our city from out of state. It was quite a stressful situation for my wife and I, it stretched us to the point of almost breaking, financially and mentally. We didn't take into consideration the fact that we had vacation time coming up and we didn't exactly know where we were going to go, or where the money was going to come from. We thought, we will just pitch a tent somewhere and call it a vacation. We were both praying and seeking the Lord, asking of Him what we should do. Two weeks before our vacation time came up, a friend of mine called me on the phone. He said, " I want you and your wife to meet my wife and I at a local family restaurant on Friday. I said okay. We didn't think much of it. When we got there he asked me a few questions. He said, " I hear your new car needs a few minor repairs in order for you guys to go on vacation". I said, " Yes". He went on to say that he and his wife wanted to pay for it, they felt the Lord prompting them to do it. I said, " Well, that's great." He said we also want to pay for your next upcoming term of ministry school and you guys a little vacation. Then he slid me an envelope across the table with $ 700 in it. We ended up going to Mackinaw City, Mi, here in the upper peninsula, fixed our car, paid for my school, and God is to be glorified. He will use anyone if you remain faithful, to bless those that love Him. It's just the way God is.

A dear friend of my wife and I is a very seasoned woman of God, and our mentor if we've ever had one. She has dealt with all kinds of personal loss and tragedy, and remained steadfast in serving God. She is currently my overseer in the youth department I serve in. She has been living on social security for over 10 years because her husband became disabled (no longer to work), with severe heart complications. She makes it on their meager little income and she has more faith in God than anyone I have ever met. Plus, she has custody of a teenage grandson whom she has raised since the age of 4 or 5, because his mother (her daughter) passed away. She is a graceful volunteer in the community and serves at our church as youth director. Just recently she had a financial miracle that was interesting to me. She was struggling financially, which hasn't been uncommon for her. She herself can't exactly get a job because she is practically on call taking care of her husband. She told the Lord that she needed a job, the lord told her, " You are working for me". She said, " Fine, then I need a raise. " The next day someone gave her a check for a thousand dollars. No joke, this is the truth I tell you.....

I recall back in 1999 when I had first started shopping around for a new truck. I had went to a local car lot and test drove a few trucks, I was really interested in this little green Chevy truck. It had few miles on it and was definitely within my price range. I liked it, but I needed to know if the Lord wanted me to have it or not. I told the dealer I would go home and give it some thought. Well, every night at home I was in the rhythm of listening to a preacher on the radio named Adrian Rogers, (who has since passed). Funny it seems, but in his message he said something to the effect, " If you are considering buying that little green truck you seen at the car lot, go ahead, that's the vehicle God wants you to have." I didn't need to ask for anyone's advice, I received my answer right then and there. I had never met that preacher, or anything, but God spoke to me through that preacher. I have had this truck for nine years (definitely worth having), and it has never left my wife or I stranded one time. And I tell you anyone who has lived in Michigan for any winter will testify, that's good news. It is just simply amazing.

I have been in ministry school for two years, and the instructors are absolutely amazing. I have had prayers answered countless times just by listening to the prophets (preachers that flow in the prophetic) . One of my instructors looked at me about eight months ago while she was " caught" up in the spirit preaching, shook her finger at me, and said, " You need to finish your book." I will say this, I have never said anything to this person about the writing of this book. So, here again God was confirming some things for me, He was encouraging me. I love Him for encouraging people. No one can lift your spirits like the Lord Jesus can...No one...

My wife and I just recently bought a new home. A little Cape Cod bungalow type of house, really quaint, but some say it is too small, but we love it. We love small, it means your family can't move in. But, the entire process of finding a home was miraculous. Our first night in this house was the most peaceful night of sleep we have ever had. The peace of God really did overtake us. After a few weeks of being here I told my wife, " Something about this house reminds me of the past, (not in a bad way though), and I just can't figure out what it is." We were out in our garage one day and I finally realized it. Our house is a block house, and the garage floor is painted a slick gray color, and I told my wife, " I've got it." Every prison cell I was in at the Iowa Mens Reformatory had this same flooring, and block walls. See, God can remind you of where He has brought you from, without condemning you. It tickled us, He has brought both my wife and I from a life of sure misery.

Tell God your specifics and let Him work out all the details of what, where,and when things in your life are supposed to work out. Remember, He knows your heart, even better than you do.

This past Christmas, 2007, my wife and I weren't really lacking in any area, we just didn't have a lot of extra cash to really spend on just she and I, mainly due to the fact that we had a minimum of 13 kids to buy presents for just in our family alone, grandkids, nieces, and nephews. However, we felt blessed, just to have our new home, and the peace of God. We were lounging around one day and my wife said to me, " Honey, I sure would like to bless some people this year just to bless them. You know, someone we don't know, just to bless them, to glorify God." I was thinking something along the same lines. I was lying in my bedroom praying one afternoon, and asked the Lord, I said, " Lord, we want to bless some people we don't even know, and Lord as you know we don't have a lot of money". Before I even finished praying my cell phone in my pants pocket rang. I answered it, it was a friend of ours. She said she was out in my driveway, and she had something to give us. I stepped outside and she handed me a card with $100 in an envelope. God is faithful. And I tell you what we did. My wife and I went to church and picked 2 names off of the angel tree, and we bought 2 children (we didn't even know) a couple of gifts a piece for Christmas. God desires to bless people. You included.....

Another true miracle that we experienced when we first got married was this. Our granddaughter who was a week old at the time went into an epilectic episode. My wife and step-daughter were at a friends house after church one Sunday having a taste-testing party. They all were lingering outside with our granddaughter being the focus of all the ladies' attention because she was a newborn. While outside they noticed as everyone was admiring her, she was having a light seizure. So, they called an ambulance. She was rushed to Devos Children's Hospital in Grand Rapids. She was diagnosed with Toxoplasmosis, a disease not really common here in the United States. It is found mainly in third world countries and it was a very trying situation for all of us. After receiving information about the disease we were told that she would more than likely be a an invalid basically. My wife and I were not going to just sit back and accept that. So, here we were in constant prayer for little Ta-Tay. It was discovered that she had a few spots on her brain from this illness, and again, statistically speaking, she didn't have much of a chance of being a normal child. The professionals told us that this is really rare, and that most of the cases in the United States are not positive. They told us that most of the patients here in the states with this disease are bedridden, and completely disabled. Today, this little girl is just as normal as can be. She is in kindergarten, and hasn't had any hospitalization or anything of that nature. Praise be to God, who has overcome the world.

Just a reminder, my wife and I are just normal everyday people. We are cut from the same mold as many of you readers. However, because we seek God, we find God. We have a whole church full of " down to earth" people who do the same. We hear what God is doing everyday, it's amazing. I tell you these things because you must understand that it is difficult to see God moving around you if you aren't seeking Him. But if you are seeking Him, you will find Him.

Just recently our church had a youth conference, revolving around the youth in the community, and the youth in our church. Our youth team, (there are 6 0f us on the team) were doing what we had to do to get ready for the weekend event. I was " moved" the Monday before the conference, I really wanted to get the speaker (our little evangelist) some new attire for the conference because he was the speaker, and he has been in between jobs lately. I asked the Lord simply, " Lord, I would like to buy my friend some clothes for this conference this weekend, will you give me the money, over and beyond what I have". I prayed it, that morning, and Tuesday morning. I didn't even tell my wife, I kinda forgot to tell her what I had petitioned the Lord for. However, I did mention it to one other friend of mine on Tuesday. I wasn't really pushing God to do anything, but I did ask Him. Friday morning rolled around, the day of our conference, and I went over to my fellow leader's home. I asked him, " What are you wearing tonight, something fancy?" He said, " Oh, I'll figure out something". I didn't breathe a word to him. I came back home, my wife and I checked the mail. We got a few junk things in the mail and a medical insurance letter that I just threw on the table. I sat down in front of the television and began reading the junk. My wife opened the medical insurance letter. She said, " Honey, there is a a check in here for $ 300". I said," Well, honey. I know where that is supposed to go." I called my friend back, and told him to get on some clothes, we were going shopping." All I have to say about this is God is faithful. The insurance company had a letter with the check stating I had overpaid last year. I don't think anymore need to be said about God blessing His people. He is as real as the shirt on my back. Thank You Lord...............

Chapter 9~
Step By Step

Once a person confesses all of their sins and wrongdoing before the Lord, things may happen in different type of cycles. I, myself, called on God two years before I actually knew what I had done. I was released from prison, then I started attending church, feeling the presence of God, and getting to know Him a little more. It's a process sometimes, but God knows exactly how to deal with each of us, and He can draw close to us at any moment. One thing I did realize was that

God was walking with me through it all, as many people know by talking to me. I know God has had a hand in my life, all along the way. He has set me free from several different bondages in my life, manic depression (or whatever they call it), prison, and lastly, myself. We learn as we walk with God, as we get to know Him more, then we have to let go of our own thoughts and plans. He will give you the desires of your heart, that's what He does. You don't even have to ask Him, He is a great God. Simply said, it is a process, to wait on anyone, much less a God you cant even see. God was doing things for me like never before, oblivious to me, but I began walking into this life that He has for me, and I wouldn't trade it for anything in the world. Don't get discouraged if you have asked God to come into your life, but you don't feel anything, or see any changes. The Bible says clearly that if you seek God you will find Him. He doesn't hide, He has no reason too. The Bible also says He is a rewarder of those who diligently seek Him.

A big point for me to make to those of you who are curious about the Lord or already walking with Him is this, don't get down on yourself when you stumble or make a mistake. No one is invincible, no one is perfect. Just get into reading your bible and fellowshipping with a church full of Christians and God will begin leading you down the path that He has for you to walk down. That's just it, some people approach people that don't know God, encouraging them to begin a relationship with God, but never show them how to seek God. Its really simple, and God is no respecter of persons. In other words, He doesn't show favoritism or push anyone away from Him.

He is desiring that all people come to Him, and develop a relationship with Him. That's His desire. And all jokes aside, everyone is seeking to fulfill a spot in their lives that only God can fill. People wander around looking for soul satisfaction, in relationships, drugs, sex, all of those things. Their souls are really longing for God. That's just the truth of it all. Yes, there are those people who know of God, but aren't willing to follow Gods guidelines, yes, He has guidelines. He is God, He is a holy God, but He will work with you, to iron out places in your life that need to be ironed out. There are even addictions in peoples lives that they cant seem to get over, you can get in a place where He can help you with those addictions. There are lots of people who have had addictions, myself included and He ironed them out. He is a God that desires for you to be free. Free of all addictions, pains, hurts, disappointments, the whole nine

yards. He has not only set me free from drugs, and alcohol, He has also set me free from soul hurts. Soul hurts; my soul was damaged as a young man from molestation by a family member. He has also set me free from shame, I have no shame. I have been cleansed from the filth that was imparted to my very soul from those deeds. He is pure, He is living water, and He cleanses His people. That is why everyone calls Him God. There are many people who come to God thinking they aren't worthy or they can't be all God wants them to be. There were many people in the bible who felt the same way, and if you begin to read it and see the bible for what it is, you'll see God worked with them. Even those who considered themselves the least. He is a restorer, that is what He does. He restores people back to himself, given them back the life that they had lost from ignorance, or just life circumstances. He is a God of hope, He is hope. He desires to bring you out of where you're at, just because you ask Him. There are many Christians today who can tell you where they were at, and where they are now in life. Lots of them. God is good to His people.

People even misrepresent God in a way that He is some sort of executioner or something, Well, He is the Judge in the End Times, on Judgement Day. But, He desires to restore you back to himself before He does bring this world to an end. He is going to judge each and every person according to their deeds on earth. Once you accept Him for who He is, Jesus stands in the gap for all those wrong doings (sins) you have committed. Jesus died for you and me, all of us . And He didn't die in vain, He died so that we can be forgiven of our sins. Jesus stands at the right of God, as an advocate, He took all the weight of our sins, so that we would be reconciled back to God. That's the gist of it folks, its simple. Don't let anyone tell you no one cares about your messed up situation you have yourself in, Jesus cares. God cares, and He desires for you to come to Him, ask Him for forgiveness, and move on. Forget your past, but learn from it. By now, you probably know what you can and cannot do to keep yourself from getting into a mess. The only part of our past we need to be concerned about is what we learned from it all. God doesn't throw my past in my face everyday reminding me about it, He has forgiven me and laid out a plan before me of what I can do in my life to please Him. He has a plan for your life too, remember that. The offer is on the table. Seek God, and He will be found, look for Him everywhere you go, and He'll find a way to speak to you. He will move on your behalf like nothing you have ever experienced before in your life, and it is a wonderful thing. Nothing can compare to having a relationship with God, nothing. Don't knock it till you've tried it.

Chapter 10~
Armageddon you say?

Yes, the Bible speaks clearly of the earth being literally destroyed in an end time war called Armaggedon. Some don't want to believe that. However, anyone with any intellect at all can see plainly that the prophecies, (predictions, if you will) of the Bible have come to pass, and many more still are going to come to pass. Why, am I telling you all this? Because you need to know. The Bible says that the Lord Jesus (God as we know Him) is coming back to earth to get His church before Armaggedon takes place. And He wants you to know. I want to be in that number. I want to be one of those people who don't have to endure the hardship of being on earth when Armaggedon takes place. The book of Revelation in the bible speaks clearly of how God himself is going to pour out His wrath upon earth. That's incredible, you say. Yes, it is not something I want to be a part of. I want to be with Him in heaven, not here on earth while people are destroying each other and God himself is showing his infuriation towards them.

I encourage you today, before you even close the backcover of this book to say that prayer that will change your life. It is a simple prayer as I've mentioned before, just be honest before God, He is everywhere, listening at all times. Then there is a process called, waiting. Allow God to move in your life, and I just know He can. This isn't a book of threats, and I hope you didn't receive it that way. I hope you gathered just what the Lord wanted you to gather, and I pray that He will show that my words herein are true, because I know what He has done in my life, and the lives of many others. He can turn your life around, for the better, I promise you.

And just be thankful you don't have to beat Him at a game of chess to be released or forgiven.

You can be Free Indeed

John 8:36